# TONGUES
# UNTIED

DIRG AAAB-RICHARDS is a poet and activist who currently works at the London Black Lesbian and Gay Centre. His poetry has appeared in *Blackout* (London) and *The Voice*.

CRAIG G. HARRIS is a native New Yorker who currently lives and writes in Washington, D.C. His writing career began in 1984 as a news reporter for the *New York Native*. Since then his essays, fiction and poetry have been published in *Au Courant*, *Bay Windows*, *Blackheart 3*, *Black/Out*, *Central Park*, *Changing Men*, *Gay Community News*, *Metro Chronicle*, *The Philadelphia Tribune*, *Point of View* and *RFD*, also in the anthologies *Gay Life* (Dolfin/Doubleday), *In The Life* (Alyson Publications) and *New Men/New Minds* (Crossing Press). He has worked in various editorial capacities at McGraw-Hill, Scholastic, Avon and Bantam Books.

ESSEX HEMPHILL is the author of *Earth Life* (1985) and *Conditions* (1986). He was awarded a 1986 Fellowship in Poetry from the National Endowment of the Arts (NEA). He is a contributor to the historic collection of literature by Black gay men, *In The Life* (1986) edited by Joseph Beam. Hemphill is also the publisher of Be Bop Books, Washington D.C., and he has been a resident of D.C. for over 20 years.

ISAAC JACKSON was the founding member of the Black gay cultural organization, Blackheart Collective which evolved into the literary magazine *Blackheart*. In addition to *Blackheart* his writing has appeared in *Gay Community News*, *The James White Review* and the anthology *Not Love Alone*.

ASSOTTO SAINT was born and raised in Haiti. He is the author of *Risin' To The Love We Need*, *New Love Song*, *Black Fag* and *Coupon Queen*, which are all theatrical pieces dealing with the lives of Black gay men. He is the lead singer of the band XOTICA, based in New York City.

GAY VERSE

# TONGUES UNTIED

*poems by*

**Dirg Aaab-Richards**
**Craig G Harris**
**Essex Hemphill**
**Isaac Jackson**
**Assotto Saint**

*Gay Verse* from GMP, the Gay Men's Press
Series Editor: Martin Humphries

Collection world copyright © 1987 GMP Publishers Ltd
Poems world copyright © 1987 Dirg Aaab-Richards,
    Craig G. Harris, Essex Hemphill, Isaac Jackson,
    Assotto Saint

This edition first published in November 1987 by
    GMP Publishers Ltd, PO Box 247, London N15 6RW,
    England

Distributed in North America by
    Alyson Publications Inc., 40 Plympton St,
    Boston, MA 02218, USA.

**British Library Cataloguing in Publication Data**

Tongues Untied: poems. – (Gay Verse).
  1. English poetry – 20th century
  2. Homosexuals' Writings
  I. Aaab-Richards, Dirg  II. Humphries, Martin
  III. Series
  821'.914'080920664      PR1178.H6

  ISBN 0-85499-053-1

Photo of Dirg Aaab-Richards by Paolo Bazzoni; of Craig G.
Harris by Sharon Farmer; of Essex Hemphill by Daniel Cima;
of Isaac Jackson by Becket Logan; of Assotto Saint by
Alcindor.
Cover photo: Rotimi Fani-Kayode from his book,
Black Male - White Male (GMP)

Printed and bound in Great Britain by
The Guernsey Press Co. Ltd., Guernsey, Channel Islands.

# Introduction

*Tongues Untied* is a reference to 'Tongue-Tied in Black and White', a poem by Michael Harper in which he expounds on how the mores and language of a dominant culture can stifle the creativity of peoples within that culture. This book is a glorious outpouring from poets who are a part of gay culture, gay traditions and also a part of Black culture and Black traditions. All of which informs, enriches, and is the seedbed of their poetry. It may be for some a language rich and strange, but for all of us it is one of mighty power and delight. It fears not the pain of experience nor the beauty of love. These five poets traverse the landscapes of their worlds with confidence and their individual voices sing out.

With great clarity all the writers share their sense and understandings of the issues confronting them as Black gay men. Common themes are the integration of racial and gender identities with gay identities; the ways in which people of colour are treated by the white world; hidden histories; magic and ritual as means of survival; homophobia; intimations of alternatives that would allow Black gay men to be free.

Each of course has his own personal vision developed from influences and traditions specific to each writer. Four of the writers are American, the experience of which deeply permeates their writing and their concerns. The fifth, Dirg Aaab-Richards, lives and works in London but his knowledge of racism only differs in specifics from that of the other poets:

> Reading works of white men,/I am
> sometimes forced/To give my credence
> to my people/My mind has to rewrite/
> What isn't there but was.

Craig G. Harris in 'Miss Lucy's Voodoo Restaurant' exposes the attitudes of 'white folks out slumming' and deftly puts the knife in:

> Miss Lucy smiled/politely and/answered
> when they/called her girl/shuffled
> back/to her kitchen/waved her
> arthritic/hands over her/Anacostia
> black/skillet/and presented her/patrons
> with/tantalizing dishes that/enflamed
> their tastebuds,/twisted their intestines,/
> and gave them the/overall appearance/
> of her day old/smothered  chicken.

Isaac Jackson in 'Prophecy' uses anecdote to illustrate the behaviour of the media:

> mama said she was gonna win/lotto
> that night and/vanessa williams was
> gonna win/and be the first black miss
> america
>
> i laughed and said if/she did win you
> would/see a sign on the screen saying:/
> 'we're sorry. we've temporarily/lost
> contact with our transmitting/station in
> atlantic city'

Essex Hemphill's poem 'Family Jewels' encapsulates a whole history in the lines:

> No matter where I live/or what I wear/
> the cabs speed by./Or they suddenly
> brake/a few feet away/spewing fumes in
> my face/to serve a fair skinned fare.

Assotto Saint in 'The Geography of Poetry' uses the story of seeking the work of a fellow poet in a bookshop to ask 'does color modify poetry?':

ntozake shange/i looked you up/among
the poets at barnes and noble/but i
didn't find you/I asked the clerk/if he
had kept you tied down/or does he use
your books/as dartboards/he smirked/
then shouted 'she's in the black
section/to the back'/even literature has
its ghettos

This also raises the question of why this book is
devoted solely to the work of black gay poets. The
answer to this is beautifully expressed by Joseph
Beam in his Introduction to *In The Life*:[1]

By mid-1983 I had grown weary of
reading literature by white gay men-
...None of them spoke to me as a Black gay
man...I called a personal moratorium on
the writing by white gay men, and read,
exclusively, work by lesbians and Black
women. At the very least, their Black
characters were credible and I caught
glimpses of my reality in their words.
...Very clearly, gay male means: white,
middle-class, youthful, nautilized, and
probably butch; there is no room for Black
gay men within the confines of this gay
pentagon.

There are many reasons for such Black gay invisibi-
lity. Hard words come to mind: power, racism,
conspiracy, oppression, and privilege – each deserv-
ing a full-fledged discussion in gay history books yet
unwritten.

*In The Life* was and is the first step towards ending
the silence that has surrounded the lives of Black gay
men. *Tongues Untied*, through being the first collec-
tion of work by Black gay poets, is a further
contribution to the ending of that silence.

One of the other major concerns of all the poets is homophobia. Not only the homophobia of a racist white community but also the homophobia of the straight Black community. The poets are unafraid of taking risks in their work and challenge the assumptions of others. Dirg is particularly clear about the homophobia within the family. And family has a different, richer meaning here from that generally understood by whites. It does not mean woman, man and 2.5 children; its meanings are concerned with community and support, sharing and loving, growth and development unconstrained by biological ties and state definitions:

> You seem tormented by the way/That I
> now express myself./When have I ever
> demanded of you/The constraints you
> desire of me?
>
> Sister, your dictate is offensive

says Dirg in 'Tell Me About Life'. Isaac writes:

> you say you don't mind/if i keep it to
> myself/so i only told my neighbor/and
> he ran and told everybody else/and
> when i got home/my house was burned
> to a shell.

The experience of homophobic violence is also explored by Craig in 'The Least of My Brothers'. He explores as well the violence within our own relationships in 'Jailhouse Rock' and 'On Beyond Masochism'. Sometimes, of course, family come through. This is related movingly in Assotto's prose poem 'Hooked For Life'. And hoped for in these lines from 'In The Life' which Essex addresses to the mothers of gay sons and lesbian daughters:

> If one of these thick-lipped/wet, black
> nights/while I'm out walking,/I find
> freedom in this village/I'll bring you
> here./And you will never notice/the
> absence of rice/and bridesmaids.

The other commonality of all the poets is their ability to write with their individual voices in ways which so clearly articulate poetically the political realities, desires and needs of being Black and gay in the United States and England. Each has a unique voice. In Dirg's writing can be seen traces of the language of Shakespeare, most obvious, to me, in his poem 'For All My Mothers' which begins: 'Sweet Afrique/Release my hidden history/Of nectar'. The theme of 'hidden history' is one which runs through all his work alongside that of the importance in affirming Black culture.

Craig explicitly explores relationships between Black gay men and the different ways we all find to live in the world and struggle for a better future. He, like Essex, questions the forms of masculinity imposed on us and celebrates the alternatives we have created for ourselves.

The poems which Essex writes are pared to the bone and sit on the page like coiled springs waiting to burst inside the reader. He performs much of his work with musician Wayson Jones, and musical qualities are inherent in the work. Essex, like all of the poets, takes risks in his choice of subject matter. His work in progress 'The Father, Son and Unholy Ghosts', in exploring the relationship between a Black gay man and his father, is challenging and questioning our received notions of what such familial ties really mean.

Music is also an important influence on Isaac's poems. The poems presented here were written in the five-year period between 1981 and 1986 and show evidence of Black musical forms like reggae, rock, rap and the blues in their structure. Isaac is also a poet who uses constant reference to the language and worlds of technology. 'Binary Black' is a rich combination of both concerns. Of all the poets here, he is the most explicit in his concern with the future and the choices we have in how that future is going to be. He also, like Assotto, sees magic and ritual as a part of everyday life, which despite technological advances is still needed to enable us to continue with our song: 'the song is unique/and perhaps the singer/but the lips and tongue/belong to all humanity' and 'we make magic/to shake off whatever was holding us down'.

Assotto uses the magic and ritual to cleanse, replace and survive. He also creates a world of shadows, dreams and memories which runs alongside that state of siege called life. It is the intermingling of the two that gives hope:

> ...the past passed on from generations,
> all the joy of life reflected. So slowly his
> body bent far forward. Long supple
> arms opened low
> to pay homage
> to surrender in payer
> to offer himself
>     a black queen      dancing with shadows
>             at high noon
> triple trouble that's brutal chasing America's
>     evil spirits away.

Martin Humphries
London, July 1987

1. *In The Life: A Black Gay Anthology*, edited by Joseph Beam, Alyson Publications, 1986.

# Dirg Aaab-Richards

## *For Black Men Who Push Pram*

Right It Now!
The World Is Flat
In Pensive Mood
For All My Mothers
Must You Deny Us All The Right
Tell Me About Life

*Acknowledgements:*
'Right It Now!' appeared in *Blackout* (London) no. 1; 'For All My
Mothers' appeared in *The Voice* and the 1985 Annual Report of
the South London Lesbian and Gay Young People's Group.

## Right It Now!

A gwine rite it down
Ah don't care what it's about
A just gwine rite it down.

Mi nah rite to nobody specific
Mi ah rite it for miself
Mi ah rite fah the
Simple joy ah doing so.

Ah don't care what it's about
It no have to say noting
It might be something happen or wish

It don't have to read
It don't have to sense
Ah just wan' rite

It can truth
It can lie – if it want
It can flounce, bounce and jounce – if it want
It can sweetly lack the intricacies of delicateness –
     if need be

Prude or rude
Ah gwine rite it
Copy it
And send it to you.

It can improve?
Say something more?
It can tidy an' type?

Moral:
It's from acorns like these that our stories get told
Use a little logic; when and to whom it is showed.

## The World Is Flat

The world is flat
This you really should know...
A white man told me so!

## In Pensive Mood

Deep in thought and
Reading works of white men,
I am sometimes forced to sift
To give my credence, to my people
My mind has to rewrite
What isn't there but was.

Truths denied
Myths subscribed
Substituted for the untruth
Which sells so easily.

Racist ramifications
Support and burrow
Deep into the mentality of the enemy.

Shrouded eyes
Negate the pigmentation
The market thrives on wicked lotions.

Enter 'DQ'
A black man is raped again
Submission; role reversed.

No orgasm can compensate
The torment thoughts
Before an understanding acquired
After years of deliberation;
Who is my mother?
Who is my father?

A sister now journeys on the
Halaperidol dreams I've had.
eager for rest – miles to go.

I listen attentively
As we make music still

Enlightened, I am elated,
Relaxed, enthralled.

I scream because myself finds me,
And they take me away.

## For All My Mothers

Sweet Afrique
Release my hidden history
Of nectar.

Blossoms of Solomon
Still grace your face
Flowers perennial
And in rebirth.

Of orchids Black
Who, in ignorance,
A generous welcome gave
Those who plundered graves
Of Kings and our writings of
Intellect devoured.

Oh dark Titania collect, collect
Bring home our share,
Reclaim your disinherited heirs

And share out among the honeycomb
This ambrosia to transform
Our drones into caring Queens.

So we might (in May) scout,
Take flight and swarm to homes
Anew; Reassured we are of you.

Blessed sod, as you decay
Give life to others so that
They may fulfill the journey in
Godspeed time.

Sharing en route with whom they choose to
     share
Lessons and skills (each a part)
So that we may not leave stones unturned
To fester till another year.

Don't delay your bloom
Flower now, time is ripe:
So each may see, again;

And when in solitude reflect
On the mysteries of this – one paradise
Where, if 'twere not for greed and lies
Enough there would be.

Oh, why do they do this to us?
See now the wretched, starving still
Arms too thin to clasp at prayer.

Each is yours O, Mother Earth
Till patience thin
Address the sin of who collude in the dreams of
     'other men'
When in melancholy
I die in shame at your sweetness, once ignored.

## Must You Deny Us All The Right

Must you deny us all the right
To 'go' with whom we choose?
Do you think it's fair, this spite?
Why are we
Born to lose?

Only more purposeful then
My lifestyle has become
Because the fight
We each must win –
For some – has not yet begun.

You lie to us on sexuality
What else is it you fear?

And angry more
I feel inside
At what you've said and done
How I oblige and
Compromise
So many songs unsung.

How then the attitudes
Of kindness you profess
Where is your understanding?...
Of all my...wretchedness?

I've often thought about how swift
And sudden
I severed and slipped away
To homes anew –
(Yet of you)
To write *my* morals for *me*!

To start afresh
Unhindered this time, *free*,
Accepting all the good things
That life has to offer me.

I've always tried to tell the truth
Which you prescribed –
What more then is required?
Would you have rather
I lived and lied?

You obviously misunderstood:
I never chose to birth in darker skin
I never chose ten fingers ten toes
I do choose to 'dress this way'
I never chose to be gay!

That cataclysmic trauma
Of my adolescent years
Which I hated and had
'twas little more than a
Warning of what could have been!
(So much unsaid, so much unseen.)

The restrictions I was applying
All those feelings I was denying:
Irresponsibly channeled,
Imagine what more damage
It could have done!

I'm sure I'll never change
The direction of
My sexual orientation
There is no switch for LEFT and RIGHT
It's a deep, deeper
Internal motivation

Do you really feel
I would deliberately
Have allowed all this agony
To occur – within myself,
Within yourselves
Lost friends,
Hours with pain?

There are other things
I'd wish a son
Who chose to go his way
I'd never wish him an unjust life
Although I might wish him gay.

## Tell Me About Life

Tell me about life
Lined with no lies.
How can we kill
And not cry?

And it's only memory I hold now
Of the times we rode together
In the dark nights home.

Yet those images from childhood
Still hold fast.
You knew the road well;
Every hairpin bend
From Nana Spring to Constant Spring
You were your own angel.

The steep slopes and sharp inclines
Of the daily journeys into town with you
Were precious times for me.

I remember the large white (man-sized) 'kerchief
I lost to the wind
As we passed somebody's banana plantation.

I'll also never forget the journeys home
When we would amuse ourselves;
Engine off, 'full stop'.
The car's head lights full on
Piercing the blackness
And watch the creatures of the night
Hop in an out of view.

The Iron River crossings sometimes scared me.
Do you remember how we nearly
Lost the Austin Morris over the edge?

We stood knee deep in the
Strong current of the day's rainfall
From the higher mountains
And you hooted the horn 'til
the nice, kind boys of Norbrook Village
Pushed the vehicle to safety
On the lower slope to our plateau.

Do you remember our week-end trips
To the sea;
Down Palisados Boulevard with a tormented
Ocean on our left and a calm harbour to the
        right...?
The day we played ring-a-ring-a-roses
As we went out deeper and deeper
Into the sea;

'The sea too full, the sea too full'
I shouted – breaking the ring,
Spluttering and running back ashore; betrayed.
Will I ever live down that line from my childhood
        years?
(Or the imagery of me flirting in crinolines?)

Do you still have the plastic farm yard
With the black and white pied bull,
The milk maid and the pig?
Have you kept the tinseled butterfly
I cut from an old christmas card?

Is there still the chiming clock
With the glass door and gargoyle's head?
Does it still mark time
With its tiny hammer?

Our lives are so rich
With so much happiness passed.

It does seem strange that my
Declaration of independence should
Affect you this way.

You seem tormented by the way
That I now express myself.
When have I ever demanded of you
The constraints you demand of me?

Sister, your dictate is offensive
And I don't care if you never ever
Discover just how very much
This man has continued to grow.

# Craig G. Harris

Inventory Time
Block Boys in BMWs
On Beyond Masochism
Sacrificial Cock
Our Dead Are Not Buried Beneath Us
The Nadir
Miss Lucy's Voodoo Restaurant
Jailhouse Rock
Rebirth
Alive After His Passion
Classified
The Least of My Brothers
The Hardening of Soft Men

*Acknowledgements:*
'On Beyond Masochism' appeared in *Black/Out*, vol. 1, no. 2;
'Sacrificial Cock' appeared in *Central Park*, no. 10, fall 1986.

## Inventory Time

The year will soon end.
My room has a new face.
Shampooed carpet and sunrise bedcovers,
Christmas cards on wrapping ribbon
hung from the curtain rod
I'm sipping beaujolais nouveau
and pumping a decade
of Joan Armatrading.
It is inventory time.
In the past year I have
done two nine to fives,
one six to two,
twenty articles,
four short stories,
three readings,
two television shows,
six men
and a lot of scotch.
I have lost
my American Express and
Visa charge privileges,
five earrings,
three contact lenses,
my mask,
two friends to AIDS,
and the innocence
of my humor.
The new year will be about
revolutions – not resolutions –
crushing myths,
building fraternities,
and loving brothers,
loving brothers,
loving brothers,
loving brothers.

December 24, 1985

# Block Boys in BMWs

*for Elias*


outside the pub
backdoor
sits another
block boy
in a BMW
custom license plates
baby shoes
strung
from rear view
mirror

his gold noose
bears a heavy cross
headlights catch a
South African
diamond
as he smiles
explaining
he only freaks
sometimes

his language
a communicable
dis – ease

## On Beyond Masochism

Forgive me.
I needed refuge
from your silent power
lighthearted intimidation
purple madness
on eastside nights
when other Bronx boys
held
slick haired
gold toothed
teen women
squeezing
their youthfulness
blue gray
and you
held me
from within
in a silk stocking ghetto

my tongue
wipes you
pure and ready
is discarded like
used tissue
is muted by your
knuckles slamming
hard
against the full
of my lips

my tongue
licks rubies
that would fall
from my chin
glimmering down the
steps of your
five floor walk up
leaving a trail
of jewels
to the bus stop

Forgive me.
I needed refuge
from the constraints
of loving you
in cramped
indigo self-pity
recurrent delusions
abbreviated ecstacy
spaces foreign
to my youth
closets I
evacuated
after adolescence.

## Sacrificial Cock

I pinch rounded buttocks
bite silver dollar nipples
hard
grind nappy pubes
against belly buttons
run my tongue tip along
stubbly adam's apples
kiss earlobes
in unfamiliar darkness
grab dreads for anchor
when my stroking
sends me reeling
uncontrollable
leaving
streams of sweet stickiness
between strangers' thighs.

Contact is topical
embraces leave me
wanting
imagining the sensations
of long ago encounters
when I allowed men
to fill my void
with pulsating rhythms
that lingered beyond
my recall
of their names
I no longer invite
strangers in
I am afraid
I am confused
I am cautious.

Drunk with cheap rum
I call on Loco Atisou
beg him to imbibe
hoping to loosen
the loa's tongue
to find the answers
the causes and the cure
but Papa Loco will not tell
I curse him
with every shortened breath
every death
each diagnosis
I no longer sing:
'Va, Loco, Loco Valadi'
offer rum libations
sacrifice my cock.

## Our Dead Are Not Buried Beneath Us

*for Marc-Steven Dear, 1953-1986*

he was older than he'd said
thinner than goodbye
slipping through airport tears
his left eye,
rebellious,
refused to yield to
weight of copper coin

his cold hands
calmly folded
accepted Laura's crystals,
Geneva's daisies
my last letter
Big Laura's last grasp

I noticed the tribal markings
of his face
multiplied
grown larger than when I'd last seen
constant reminders of
dimly lit liaisons

the lid closed
on so much unfinished business
in the appropriate absence
of a father who might
have loved a son too dark,
too precious
and the presence
of a man who tried.

# The Nadir

*for Steven*

It is now three years,
two relationships,
fourteen fleeting affairs,
and seventeen tricks later.
I come to you late at night
disorientated, disconnected, needing...
you allow me to become a little boy
      again
tracing the outline of your beard,
unbuttoning your pyjama top
to tug at your chest hair,
you tell me this affectionate play
is something you're no longer accustomed to
I ask about your lover,
he doesn't give you what you need,
you don't give me what I want,
and I don't give a damn about him
because in this life,
I have found that I need you,
after two relationships,
fourteen fleeting affairs,
and seventeen tricks,
to tell me it's alright,
bring me apple juice in bed,
hold me,
let me lick the nicotine
from your teeth,
and draw close to you
while you sleep.

## Miss Lucy's Voodoo Restaurant

Miss Lucy
took very little
shit
from white folks
at her small time
greasy spoon
good cookin'
restaurant
just far enough
from anything
including West Hell
to make young professionals
think it chi-chi.

Miss Lucy served up
pickled watermelon rinds
wrapped in bacon,
she crab soup,
boudin puddin',
mamou coush-coush,
fever in the kitchen
and more than a few
smart mouthed
white folks
out slumming
for the evening.

Miss Lucy smiled
politely and
answered when they
called her girl
shuffled back
to her kitchen
waved her arthritic
hands over her
Anacostia black
skillet
and presented her
patrons with
tantalizing dishes that
enflamed their tastebuds,
twisted their intestines,
and gave them the
overall appearance
of her day old
smothered chicken.

Miss Lucy is my girl
but don't mess with her,
a post-modern Petro,
she'll slap your effigy
in her microwave
and press 3 –
fry.

## Jailhouse Rock

steel shadow stripes
color the cot –
the moment of
circumstantial closeness
threatening death

acting with
violent passion
the rapist
does not pause
to protect his
victim
with smuggled
contrabrand

track marks
tattoo the forearm
that blocks scream
and easy breath
at the neck

the completed act
leaves contaminated
blood
on government sheets
and the faint sounds
of manchild tears.

## Rebirth

*for Eugene*


his brotherlove
touches me
like a woman
stroking
her pregnant belly,
calming the restlessness
within darkness,
the anxiety
of future world
unknown.

he welcomes
the subtle pains
my existence brings
with fearful anticipation
of the day
our cord is broken
by miles, time zones
and work to be done.

I am rocked
in buoyant
waves of his
affection
and momentarily,
comfortably,
abandon the fight
to reap benefits
of battles won.

# Alive After His Passion

*for Elias*

green mangos
with salt and
vinegar
hearts of palm
and holy ghosts
make me
speak in
tongues
with garlic breath,
dance to unheard
beats
fall beneath your
holy temple
inhaling gray
incense dust,
writhing in
shed snake skins
purified in the
flame,
wrapped
in unspeakable
joy.

## Classified

BGA* 30ish
well-read
sensitive
pro-feminist
seeks same for
envelope licking,
flyer distribution,
banner assembly,
demonstration companion,
dialogical theorizing,
good times,
and hot safe sex.

Why do we go home alone,
clutch pillows and journals
in single beds,
push ourselves to the nth degree
for the cause
if we can't reap the benefits?

I do not
want to wed the movement,
do you?
End the silence baby.
We could make
a serious revolution
together.

*Black Gay Activist

## The Least of My Brothers

summer full moon night started
with the rhetorical chant,
'Hey faggot, what you doing around here?'
city rocks fell around
his quickened footsteps,
a wad of spit flew to his bare shoulder,
empty coke bottle
cracked against trash can rim,
sparkling jagged edges
motioned for his throat,
a blackjack knocked him unconscious,
his money and ID removed,
his face slashed, disfigured

left in a bloody pool
he waited for the police, ambulance,
the kindness of brethren,
or Jesus to pick up his messages.

## The Hardening of Soft Men

*for Richard Bruce Nugent*

Lily hits streets
in purple pumps
with sturdy shaved
legs revealed
in sheer stockings
selling whatever
boys buy
on sweaty nights
when no one's
watching

Jade graces stages
in glittered gowns
mouths melodies
to dance steps
rehearsed before
broken mirrors
or singles shoved
between brassiere
cups and
deception
stiletto tongue
staccato curses
spit in
Spanish at
strangers who
signal the
lump at her
throat,
the stubble
at her cheeks
drunken appreciation
drawled blessings
descend on audiences
who applaud
the dramatic flare
of her performance
the identical
appearance and mannerisms
of the reigning
disco diva
Lily counts tens
from jobs blown
under steering wheels,
public trees,
half moons
that turn to
sunrise before
the close of
business and
midday rest

Jade counts bars,
measures,
hit singles,
scratched
twelve inches,
checks
lip synch,
lip stick,
minutes to
showtime.

her bestowal of
gratuities selfless
undaunted by fear
of violence or arrest
she does not
seek affection
on steamy streetcorners
it is the hardening
of soft men
she desires

her performance
delivered with pride
her message filled
with encouragement
she does not
seek acceptance
on smokey stages
it is the hardening
of soft men
she desires

# Essex Hemphill

## *Red Annie vs The United States*

*for the Queen of Soul*

*Acknowledgements:*
'Black Beans' is reprinted from *Earth Life*, published by Be Bop Books, Washington D.C., 1985.
'American Wedding' and 'In the Life' are reprinted from *Conditions*, published by Be Bop Books, Washington D.C., 1986.

## Family Jewels

*for Washington D.C.*


I live in a town
where pretense and bone structure
prevail as credentials
of status and beauty.
A town bewitched
by mirrors, horoscopes
and corruption.

I intrude on this nightmare.
Arm outstretched from curbside.
I'm not pointing to Zimbabwe.
I want a cab
to take me to Southeast
so I can visit my mother.
I'm not ashamed to cross
the bridge that takes me there.

No matter where I live
or what I wear
the cabs speed by.
Or they suddenly brake
a few feet away
spewing fumes in my face
to serve a fair skinned fare.
I live in a town
where everyone is afraid
of the dark.
I stand my ground unarmed
facing a mounting disrespect,
a diminishing patience,
a need for defense.

In passing headlights
I appear to be a criminal.
I'm a weird looking muthafucka.
Shaggy green hair sprouts all over me.
My shoulders hunch and bulge. I growl
as blood drips from my glinting fangs.

My mother's flowers are wilting
while I wait.
Our dinner
is cold by now.

I live in a town
where pretense and structure
are devices of cruelty.
A town bewitched
by mirrors, horoscopes
and blood.

## Etc. Etc. Etc.

I ride home shedding tension.
Crammed into a five o'clock tube.
Dodging briefcases, odd-sized purses,
knapsacks filled with study.

I gaze homeward in muted silence,
kind of blue, anxious to transfer.
A different train, another bus
will complete the journey to sanctuary.

At the end of the line,
departing the bus,
I walk through the blocks
stepping over bodies.
Or I stop to examine them
like a species of flowers
that thrive in western climates.
Faces pressed against the concrete.
A vile nectar clings to their lips.
They crawl along the pavements
trembling, tentative vines.

Deflowered by a winter
that rages cruelly
inside each of them.
A white squall
that howls at their hearts
shattering the black moon
that rocks there
full of wishes.
Defenseless.

If they were elephants,
they would have gone off
alone
by now.

## Overtones

There will always be nuisance.
Or I could let myself be captured
by the magic flute of satyrs
who would gently lure me to entrapment
to drink my blood
for one more day of life.

If in my substance
it could be conveyed
how little I give a damn about tomorrow,
the length of my trousers,
the circumcision I didn't agree to,
the daily shave, the score, the mythology.
Would they be shocked to discover
contempt clinging to my cells like algae.

Nuisance: dying to assuage insanity.
Religious fervour. Moral pandemonium.
The unexpected lurks near the hours
you thought private.
What will you accept
in exchange for your silence?
What life do you want
for one more day?

If it's a better vision
let's die here, a soldier's death,
the death of tulips – and spring.
If blood and flesh will win us
a new world that is not a token
or a statue covered in pigeon shit.

## Skin Catch Fire

*for Dennis*


In the very old sorrow of London,
beneath gull scarred skies
as raped cultures rise
to accuse and curse the crown,
in the drear light
sorrow casts over decay,
I leave you, in the care
of ancient snakes with ears.
I leave you in the lonely graffiti of:
'Smack keeps us warm
and we are loved'.

What will keep us warm?
A tender, burning nipple?
A gentle contusion on the neck
where we bit too hard
or sucked too long?
Will it be this memory
which guides our hands
along our thighs
to the rod of questions?

I leave you the power of hope
for a sane salvation.
Use it like bread,
trust it like a vow.
Beneath gull scarred skies
I leave. My laughter, a falcon
climbing above misery,
concealed in air.
it reaches your ears
as your name
touches my lips
causing my skin

to catch fire
like a city,
a phoenix,
a pyromantic.


## Black Beans


Times are lean
Pretty Baby,
the beans are burnt
to the bottom
of the battered pot.
Let's make fierce love
on the overstuffed
hand-me-down sofa.
We can burn it up, too.
Our hungers will evaporate
like money.
I smell your lust,
not the pot burnt black
with tonight's meager meal.
So we can't buy flowers for our table.
Our kisses are petals,
our tongues caress the bloom.
Who dares to tell us
we are poor and powerless?
We keep treasure
any king would count as dear.

Come on, Pretty Baby.
Our souls can't be crushed
like cats crossing streets too soon.
Let the beans burn all night long.
Our chipped water glasses are filled
with wine from our loving.
And the burnt black beans –
caviar.

## American Wedding, 1986

In america
I place my ring
on your cock
where it belongs.
No horsemen
bearing terror,
no soldiers of doom
will swoop in
and sweep us apart.
They're too busy
looting the land
to watch us.
They don't know
we need each other
critically.
They expect us to call in sick,
watch television all night,
die by our own hands.
They don't know
we are becoming powerful.
Every time we kiss
we confirm the new world coming.

What the rose whispers
before blooming
I vow to you.
I give you my heart,
a safe house.
I give you promises other than
milk, honey, liberty.
I assume you will always
be a free man with a dream.
In america,
I place your ring
on my cock
where it belongs.
Long may we live
to free this dream.

# The Father, Son and Unholy Ghosts

### i

We are not always
the bravest sons
our fathers dream.
Nor do they always
dream of us.
We don't always
recognize him
if we have never
seen his face.
We are suspicious
of strangers.
Question:
is he the one?

### ii

I stand waist deep
in the decadence of forgetting.
The vain act of looking the other way.
Insisting there can be peace
and fecundity without confrontation.
The nagging question of blood hounds me.
How do I honor it?

### iii

I don't understand
our choice of angers,
your domestic violence,
my flaring temper.
I wanted tenderness
to belong to us
more than food or money.

The ghost of my wants
is many things:
lover, guardian angel,
key to our secrets,
the dogs we let sleep.
The rhythm of silence
we do not disturb.

iv

I circle questions of blood.
I give a fierce fire dance.
The flames call me.
It is safe. I leap
unprepared to be brave. I surrender
more frightened of being alone.
I have to do this
to stay alive.
To be acknowledged.
Fire calls. I slither
to the flames
to become birth.

v

A black hole, gaseous,
blisters around its edge,
swallows our estranged years.
They will never return
except as frightening remembrances
when we are locked in closets
and cannot breathe or scream.

I want to be free, daddy,
of the black hole between us.
The typical black hole.
If we let it be
it will widen enough

to swallow us.
Won't it?

*vi*

In my loneliest gestures
learning to live
with less is less.
I forstalled my destiny.
I never wanted
to be your son.
You never
made the choice
to be my father.
What we have learned
from no text book;
is how to live without
one another.
How to evade the stainless truth.
Drug pain bleary-eyed.
Harmless.
Store our waste in tombs
beneath the heart,
knowing at any moment
it could leak out.
And do we expect to survive?
What are we prepared for?
Trenched off.
Communications down.
Angry in alien tongues.
We use extreme weapons
to ward off one another.
Some nights, our opposing reports
are heard as we dream.
Silence is the deadliest weapon.
We both use it.
Precisely.
Often.

## In The Life

Mother, do you know
I roam alone at night
wearing colognes,
tight pants,
chains of gold.
Searching for men
willing to come back
to candlelight.
I'm not scared of these men
though some are killers
of sons like me.
I learned
there is no tender mercy
for men of color,
for sons who love men
like me.

Do not feel shame for how I live.
I chose this tribe
of warriors and outlaws.
Do not feel you failed
some test of motherhood.
My life has borne fruit
no woman could have given me
anyway.

If one of these thick-lipped
wet, black nights
while I'm out walking,
I find freedom in this village.
If I can take it with my tribe
I'll bring you here.
And you will never notice
the absence of rice
and bridesmaids.

## Holidays

We sleep in separate bedrooms
during her visit.
I become your tenant.
You – my landlord.
We perform
until she is driven
to the airport.
Kissed away by her dutiful son.
The insufferable holiday is over:
I hang the mirror above our bed
where it always is. You screw
the red light into the lamp.
We discard our clothes, our masks.
We fumble like strangers.
The heavy breathing of criminals
entraps us: between guilt and love
with only enough courage in our blood
to get our dicks hard
like every other night before.


## Red Annie vs the United States

I should have been queen.
No one tried to encourage me.
I was likely to be laughed at
or beaten black and blue
by blockboys who didn't care
for my flavor.
But that was alright.
I didn't care for theirs.

I began stepping out with a switchblade.
It took slashing two punks in the face
to convince them
I was not to be fucked with.

I wanted to be a woman.
Not somebody's wench or door mat.
I was on a journey
to find the spirit
of the woman in me.

I was willing to let go my penis,
a man's most prized possession.

Some men don't realize
they have a soul
until their penis
is in hand. The hard
evidence of existence
I could live without.

I will always be a freak
for this reason.
An outsider of either sex.
But when he comes over
to kiss my weary shoulders,
when he comes
there are no rebellions.
No resistance.

All the neighbors know
he's visiting. When he leaves
their excitment through thin walls fades.
The ordinary dissonance of any city resumes,
where a woman like myself,
living an affair with a married man
sleeps peacefully, free of the ring,
the duties and sorrows of his hand.

## American Hero

I have nothing to lose tonight.
All my men surround me, panting,
as I spin the ball above our heads
on my middle finger.
It's a shimmering club light
and I'm dancing, slick in my sweat.
Squinting, I aim at the hole
fifty feet away. I let the tension go.
Shoot for the net. Choke it.
I never hear the ball
slap the blackboard. I slam it
through the net. The crowd goes wild
for our win. I scored
thirty-two points this game
and they love me for it.
Everyone of them is hollering
is a friend tonight.
But there are towns,
certain neighborhoods
where I'd be hard pressed
to hear them cheer
if I move on the block.

# Isaac Jackson

milk with a trace of acid
scarves and headbands (paradise
    garage '81)
prophecy
aids vigil
the birds and the bees (blues poem)
the ring
mau mau man
fine tuning for fleshtones (porno rap)
radio control room
memorandum
binary black
blueberry jam
introducing
song to whitman
for buchi
brown dream #1
endure
electrical fire
children
mice
michael stewart is dead

*Acknowledgements:*
'michael stewart is dead' has previously appeared in *Blackheart
2: The Prison Issue*, Blackheart (Black Gay Men's Press) and *Not
Love Alone: a modern gay anthology*, edited by Martin Humphries,
GMP 1985.

## milk with a trace of acid

*for dean*

y'know i wanted to kiss you
but i was already scared for you
being alone, jewish and a faggot
the cover of the new york native
blaring boy buns from your lap
across the bronx bound #4

i'm lifting weights now
last summer this guy
pulled a knife on me
in the train
screaming about my dreads and glasses

i guess we all need some contacts
something to make us blend in
with the scenery
the neighborhoods in new york
we cannot walk through
as long as there's always
an angry mob for gays and blacks
these feelings must be vomited up

oh yeah
thank you for the homemade
bread & cookies
it was wonderful to taste you
as i drank the milk
while the butter ran
down the corner of my mouth
washing away any trace of acid

## scarves and headbands
## (paradise garage '81)


you are a cyborg
part machine part animal

if it's too cold outside
your batteries freeze

inside is a streetside equator
hot like a fire engine (and just as loud)
thousands of men dancing
time for an emergency exit
TOOT TOOT lets go!
there's even room to space out in
the Monkey Room
where time is fun
doing time is instep
doing time is worship

so chill out
heat sounds like
pressure cooking

## *prophecy*

mama said she was gonna win
lotto that night and
vanessa williams was gonna win
and be the first black miss america

i laughed and said if
she did win you would
see a sign on the screen saying:
'we're sorry. we've temporarily
lost contact with our transmitting
station in atlantic city'

we did see her crowned though
much to my surprise
but mama warned her
through the tv
to be careful of people
putting something in her drink
to slur her speech

## *aids vigil*

my hope
my life
mocked by the light of a candle

the men came
one by one to the microphone
to tell us their stories
of hope that bounced
off the granite walls
in the empty space
that is the center of washington, dc

the loudspeakers appealing to
the building high statues of
dead presidents
asking them to hope with us
might as well been a radio wave
bounced off the bottom of a
lunar sea

my hope
my life
mocked by the light of a candle

holding hands at the aids vigil
listening to the testimonies
hearing the wind as breath
that will blow this candle out

## the birds and bees (blues poem)

preacher man has visions
but he can't see me
politicians make decisions
but they don't ask me
and all the colors of the rainbow
don't come clearly on my tv

whats that saying about not
seeing the forest for the trees
whats that saying about not
seeing the forest for the trees
well you can't see the sex
for the heterosexuality

forget about the bees
the birds are all we need
won't you say that you are gay
and fall in love with me
'cos the birds eat the seeds
and then they shit out the trees
i wonder what would happen if
i got down on my knees?

they'll try and tell you
love is an arrow that pierces the heart
and life is for working
every single day until you drop
and sex is for babies or
the human race would stop

you say you don't mind
if i keep it to myself
so i only told my neighbor
and he ran and told everybody else
and when i got home
my house was burned to a shell

forget about the bees
the birds are all we need
won't you say that you are gay
and fall in love with me
'cos the birds eat the seeds
and then they shit out the trees
i wonder what would happen
if i got down on my knees?


## *the ring*


the man who will love me
his ring is made of
                carrots, kisses and safesex
his ring is made of clouds, lines, whiskers and
                fingernails

you will look at our love
as you see my poetry or my hair
without value
not knowing whether or not
it has been combed

## *mau mau man*

mau mau man dug a hole in the ground
and you know he's not crazy
mau mau man dug a hole in the ground
and he's not planting daisies

put your dreams in the earth
soon they will grow out of the dirt
stick your feet in the sea
mountains will move eventually

mau mau man dug a hole in the ground
and you know he's not crazy
mau mau man dug a hole in the ground
and he's not planting daisies

children, this you should know
plant in the starlight
and your juju will grow
stick your hands in the fire
if you burn we know you're a liar

mau mau man dug a hole in the ground
and you know he's not crazy
mau mau man dug a hole in the ground
and he's not planting daisies

seeing he moon in the sky
changing phases marking lines
open the palms of your hands
mau mau man will let you understand

## fine tuning for fleshtones (porno rap)

lester was in prison
since he was a teen
had no future
no self-esteem
the man made him a star
put his photo
in all of the bars
fade to black
fade to grey
they never discussed it
they had nothing to say
to each other
the poor brother
the man controlled the sound
made sure the magazines got around

lester went back to prison
came out looking too old
but his preference for the covers
didn't grow cold
but the man had
younger trade and wasn't impressed
so lester pumped three bullets
into his chest
only thing missing
was the photos from the desk

it was a bank robbery
from an image bank
it's an image war
and our bodies are tanks
images stop time
but don't y'know
it's the age of flesh
and the age of bones

## radio control room

old timers at my door
intercom is the censor
so call me up
don't ring my bell

i'm so involved at the moment
that i might miss my cue
whatever happen to
guitar playing milton nascimento
underneath my window

reproduction rugs
woven with computer hands
people reading ticker tape
as if they understand

what all the numbers mean
its all a crazy scheme
they're putting submarines into the sea
aiming bombs at you
aiming bombs at me

sometimes i dream

i'm in the radio control room
and i hear the ebs*
and then i awake into my own room
and i realize
it was only a test


* ebs is the emergency broadcast system that all radio
stations use for communications 'in the event of a nuclear
attack'.

# *memorandum*

we spent the winter plotting
you were going to mexico
i would finish school and meet you there
i got jealous of past loves
you shaved i didn't like it
till you kissed me and rubbed
your stubborn face on mine

i fried us some chicken
lit a candle for the new year
played 'planet waves' by dylan
'on a night like this'
the candles burned down low
we danced drunk on wine

i was patient while you painted
all night then got under
the covers to cover me
i was fixated by your colors
and you by mine
we fought sometimes
and you usually let me win
i cried when your train pulled out
a big long cry

i wrote you every week
i moved in with a texan
you were jealous
i assured you it was platonic
i moved out when he showed me
his dick

i had an operation
i bled all night and in the morning
but i was sick
mostly for you

your letters from mexico came painted
my mother withdrew her money for the trip
i cleaned toilets for airfare
only job a black teenager could find in a week
you couldn't tell your patrons about me
i saved the money and told you i was coming
you sent me money for supplies
i struggled with stretchers
all the way to oaxaca

on the train down from mexico city
i was afraid but full of hope
the wooden train caught fire
my head rushed full of nightmares
dying in flames to meet you
too romantic a fate for a kid from queens
the train went faster and the flames died out

we lived together in the mountains
surrounded by corn and wild turkeys
and indian women who taught me how
to wash clothes by the river on
        the stones
the children ran behind me kicking dust
wanting to touch my african hair
for the first time

the summer ended and i lit a fire
with twigs a little boy brought me
for the hot water in the shower
i had to go back to school
you had to get your paintings ready
for your show and your patron

back in new york
i slept on the floor
of a loft and became a vegetarian
six months later you were back
we went out to eat
i ate a hamburger
and got sick
you laughed at me and told me
we weren't lovers anymore
and i never saw you again


## *binary black*


between one and zero
off and on
            not the absence of
            or the combination of
            all the colors
but binary
between one and zero
off and on

between con and verse
scanning for meaning
around where the tongue meets
the roof of your mouth

where the beat becomes digital
and all the strains
get to be code
on a chip
near the tip of your tongue

### blueberry jam (for arthur)

making blueberry jam
stirring
thinking of you
your hair and smile
melting down into a fleshy
            hunk of man, sweaty
underneath my chest

blueberry jam
how i love you
smelling sweet

### introducing

from dance
i learned that numbers
come from the earth
ground zero

from rock and roll
i learned that the riddims i like
come from Africa
the launching pad

from poetry
i learned to make images of my own
the magic
was always there
sounding spirits with a
snake wind

## song to whitman

rub my beard
across the sky
wash the chewing gum
outta my eyes
o whitman
o great one
ancient song of myself

stay soft for me
inside my balls
come out
laughing
ejaculating
sticky pine puss verse
drawn to the sun
in redwood motion
my lip hangs down in admiration
gently, close it
with a kiss

only that will
stop my mind
start my heart
beating

## for buchi

in the notes of your song

for the first time
i have discovered my own weary blues
welfare mother novelist
i can hear you
all the way out here
on staten island
where trees bristle
and dog sirens cry
at the faintest footsteps
our typewriter sounds
are often mistaken for

your children are asleep
            so is my lover
now we find time to write
we both worked that can of beans
            for a meal
our loved ones are satisfied
are we?

growing wild on this soil
of north america
another night not in his arms
our tempers grow short
no one made time for us
and we sacrifice
the money, the movies, the walk
on the promenade watching idle ships

the late night poet
cannot breathe
without the light in the bathroom
leave it on

## brown dream #1

i have this recurrent dream
of falling in love with a poet
like langston hughes
who would know the satisfaction of words
thrown across a space
acoustic or screen
or page dead white

both our minds would move in
circular 19th century motion
riding the trains up an downtown
living in a brownstone
in some port city
sea level pressure on our hads
driving us harbour crazy

rejoice and dig our oil, hair
and philharmonic bounty
swung in piano boogie concertos

## *endure*

we make magic
so this will pass over i & i
we make magic
to shake off whatever was holding us down
whatever was stuck to our wings
whatever was making the young old
and the old like they'd never
been children

we are the ones
black gay men
we are the ones
who are truly not afraid of life
for we have a deep sense
of the ways of the world
and respect her mysteries

our spells unite the goddess aspect
with our lightning rod
go sweet honey gatherers, stowaways
and ethiopian monks
endure endure
this song rises out of dust
each generation
can't fight this forceful vibe
every nation has a dust bowl
but every person doesn't have a nation
for some the planet is enough

## electrical fire

its alright
to acquiesce to
the demands of a people
whose history has been
undone
whose dreams
are not dead

when you have to be a poet
or else you and your people will die
its alright
to hear the demands of a sister
who has never heard her
brother before
the father whose son
to him is not a man

muscles coiling in defense
don't fight the blood
acquiesce to the demands
of your people

everybody has sex organs
blacks have no claim on that
what is truly black
is not nesting in my crotch
unwanted parasites

your itching is not feeling
your scratching is only that
pain without understanding
bigotry homophobia lies & silence

the song is unique
and perhaps the singer
but the lips and tongue
belong to all humanity
don't you dare tell me
what to do with them
ever
yeah
its alright to say that

i don't know any other way
to say it
i can't see the wisdom in
writing cool collected prose
like virginia woolf wrote before the war
the nazis came anyway
don't wait for the storm troopers
to recognize the fascism within us all

fascism is like an
electrical fire
burns
inside the wall
slow
stinky
our nerve endings seem the same
but further up
before the brain
the fire grows
burning hatred uncontrolled

your itching is no feeling
it is the electrical fire inside
you feel
where no one sees
until it is too late

black people
extinguish it
distinguish it
from what is really black
don't wait
the fire this time
the smoke itself will kill you

## *children*

i recognize children as
the spiritual beings
they are

they like to:
hug
play
laugh
stick fingers in jars
faces lit green
from computer screens
circles from triangles

# *mice*

mice
mice
poor little mice
no one must like you
my little friends
or why would they make you puff our
nasty cigarettes all day
and get daily injections of DES, EDB, DDT
nutrasweet and asbestos and
why, why
would anybody make you sniff poppers?
to see if you become immune suppressed?
followed by forced starvation to see how long
it would take for you to eat your young

mice
mice
dark furry mammal
your hungry legions warn the world
could they would rid you from the cities
in one raging fireball or
starve you
mice
mice
poor little mice
no one must like you
my little friends

## michael stewart is dead

(Michael Stewart was brutally murdered by New York City
transit police in the fall of 1983. His eyes were removed and
destroyed illegally by the coroner's office to prevent justice
from being brought to bear on the guilty transit policemen.
Michael Stewart worked as a busboy in the Pyramid Club, a
gay-owned and operated club on Manhattan's Lower East
Side.)


on the number one/going downtown to the
garage/ two white cops/standin' in front of me/
description of crimes and suspects/blare out/
of his box/offending my sense/if it was my radio/
i'd get a ticket.

one sez to the other: wouldn't it be funny if/
when a call went out/the guy was sitting right in
front of you/wouldn't it be funny/and easy to do/
two against one/two hands against a gun/
it could have been me.

i waz living on the lower east side/a few blocks
from the pyramid/when i first noticed him/
picking up empty beer glasses/pushing thru
the mixed crowd/gays/lesbians/straights/
bridge & tunnel crowd/shoulder to shoulder w/
east village artists/thin dreads hanging into his
eyes/i often commented to friends i might
consider trimming my dreads like his/
long in front/short on the sides/like the black guy
in/The Thompson Twins/'Hush my baby...
don't you cry...we have one weapon in our
defense/silence'/

at the fourteen street stop/on the 11 line/
doing my art in the subways/drawing sketches/
influenced by graffiti art/left no marks on the
walls/anywhere/working hard/sketching the
Statue of Liberty/leading the people/to some
billboard Liberia/i'm doing this sketch for the
anti-gentrification show/and this transit worker
gets irate/and rips my painting/to shreads/
Miz Liberty to shreads/screams/yells/tears/
i walk away/and live to complain.

i never knew his name before/i learned it by
reading in the paper/of the death of a young
man/ a young dread-locked graffiti artist/
in the custody of transit police/following an
        arrest.

Michael Stewart is dead/and wouldn't it be
funny/if the suspect/waz already standing in
front of you/and easy to do two against one/
two hands against a gun/it could have been me/
this time i got away.

# Assotto Saint

## *Triple Trouble*

It occurs to me that I am America.
*Allen Ginsberg*

*To Ortez Alderson, Willie C. Barnes and Carl Morse*

Soul
Carbon Copy
Something Just Meant to Be
Ghosts
I Want to Celebrate
Sacrifice
Widower
State of Siege
The Geography of Poetry
Shores
Hooked for Life
Epitaph
Triple Trouble

*Acknowledgements:*
Some of these poems were published in the following periodicals:
*Changing Men, RFD, Black Out* and *Other Countries.*

## Soul

i remember the beginning
a dream ancient as dawn
a dream of destiny drumming up
the blood
our flesh
this earth
a dream we were once one
soul

## Carbon Copy

as with so many of us
father was never there
but daddy
your shadow's everywhere
you are this immense black sun
i aspire to
all i breathe is fog
from those precious pictures
mother kept
i am your carbon copy
america is full of slick black cats
whose big dicks sire bastards
america is full of black bastards
who dream of daddy's big dick
how i wait
anywhere
wait
for the day we meet
i shall kiss
blow you
muthah-fuckah
away

## Something Just Meant to Be

often
trying to rid myself of
this black gay image
i galloped after the alternative
like a harnessed horse collapsed
in draft apologies foamed
at the mouth bitter

one morning
in the catskills i looked at
the sun
              the birds
the trees
              the river
myself

ever since
i ride on life
just as i am
hungry for ground
i eat this black gay nitty gritty
whole in its elements
something just meant to be


## Ghosts

both posed
in the backroom's shadows
caught
in memories of promises
kisses
some sunrise long ago
yet
neither said hello

## I Want to Celebrate

i want to celebrate vicious officious cocks
that kind with a hook or mushroom head
cast spells
made me lose consciousness when most alive
forced to acquiesce
grace under pressure
holiness in being truly low

i want to celebrate cushiony groins
hot balls a mouthful
tough titties with clip marks
hairy fists armed with a magic twist
which knew no limits
& this well-greased ass here
took pleasure in its added dimensions

i want to celebrate masters worshipped whole
top-training tricks kicks & licks
all those last calls
a stranger's smile posed no danger
then in my instinct i trusted
a past i ransack
now my conscience & my hands are my best
        friends

## Sacrifice

we wanted wine
the simple charm of a bottle
the toasts
the bouquet
a melody for memory
our fears never faded with a kiss
there's madness this moment
the bottle falls
in a ritual of threats
sharp shards cut
we are suckers for each other's
spilled blood


## Widower

*for jim*

his is the pain that blots
then suffocates
memories crush thoughts into choked words
silent screams pant for wind
every step heaves heavy
time tolls
one
his is the pain which cannot stop
till he falls
too

## State of Siege

Nile is often startled out of deep sleep when someone steps on the grate: cat jumps out of a garbage can, kids crash beer bottles, even when the window rattles in the wind, he is so startled that he gasps for breath as if all the air blew out of him. In a flash, he pulls out the nine-inch knife under his pillow. He sits on the bed, straight, still. He waits twenty minutes; an hour or two; many times until daybreak, when he kisses the knife softly, puts it back under his pillow, rolls up his body like a ball, crawling into himself, alone with memories of that night – so long ago now – like many New York City August nights, treacherous.

No air-conditioner and no fan, the heat made him twist in bed. He got up about midnight, changed the sweat-drenched sheets, pulled up the shades, opened wide the fire-escape window – the only window in the bedroom – even a breeze was a hard bargain to wish for but at least he could view the full moon; toast it with cheap white wine. Nile lay naked. Dreams beamed down.

Suddenly he felt fingers lock around his neck. He panicked and tried to scream but the fingers were choking him. He kicked mad, pushed the attacker aside, knelt on the bed, looked for anything to whack the attacker's head with when he heard him growl: 'If you make one more move, I'll can your fuckin' face, you little faggot.' The attacker hammered his foot into Nile's spine, pinning him down on the bed while he twisted his arms behind his back.

'Yeah, I been watchin' you wiggle your faggot's ass,' he said, 'walkin' with them airs. I been wantin' that piece sometime now.'

Nile couldn't move so he slightly turned his head to look at his attacker. All he saw was a big body. Moist glistening eyes peered out of a dark ski mask. He smelled whiskey. That look frightened him most. Nile trembled.

'I told you don't move,' the attacker yelled, back-handed him across the head. Smack.

Nile's jaw cracked. He coughed out three teeth and kept moaning 'Take anything you want just don't hurt me. Please.'

The attacker kept yelling, 'Bitch, I told you be quiet. Shut up.' Smack. 'Shut your stupid mouth little faggot. Shut up.' Smack. 'Now you really gettin' my juice flowin. I'm gonna stick it to you good.'

The attacker bit him hard on the ass. Nile screamed. The attacker grabbed the pillow, put it all over his head, spread-eagled him, lunged and plunged. Muffled cries...stifled sighs...

Hours later when he woke up – blood seeping out of his broken nose, blood seeping out of his twisted lips – Nile tried to stand up but his knees buckled. He couldn't walk. He couldn't talk. He dragged himself slowly across the floor to the window, climbed on the sill and passed out again.

At Bellevue Hospital, someone told him some school-girl had seen his naked body hanging on the fire-escape, a wine bottle sticking out of his ass and had called the cops.

Ever since, every night, he checks the double locks on the door. He checks that the window is shut tight. He checks that the nine-inch knife is where it must be and Nile slips into this state of siege.

## The Geography of Poetry

*for ntozake shange*

ntozake shange
i looked you up
among the poets at barnes & noble
but i didn't find you
walt was there amidst leaves of grass
anne gazed down
her glazed eyes dreamt of rowing & mercy
erica posed in her latest erotica
even rod took much space
i searched among ghosts
& those alive
still i didn't find you
i asked the clerk
if he had kept you tied down
or does he use your books
as dartboards
he smirked
then shouted 'she's in the black section
to the back'
even literature has its ghettos
stacked
amongst langston nikki & countee
maya who looked mad
the blues had her bad
zake tell me
did you demand to be segregated
does color modify poetry
i asked the manager
he patted me
whispered
'it's always been this way'

## Shores

i remember
makkis sailing the aegean sea
on breakfast of feta baklava & sunshine
pepe rafting through floating gardens
a siesta of mariachi & margaritas
abdullah who sliced the golden nile
with his felucca
bits of pita beans broken english
falling from his lips
olive-skinned mario of the gondolas
who enchanted with pasta pasolini stars
kisses them arrivederci
they chattered about anchoring their dreams
on america's shores
they ought to know
our lady in the harbour
milks immigrants
of the honey in their blood


## Hooked for Life

There were no tears. There was no time for tears
that year. Just a tight knot in the pit of my chest
where it hurts more each day. Yet, it had all
come to this: a two-pound plastic bag filled with
ash, bits of bone, fragments of teeth that didn't
completely burn. It had all come too quickly.

It seems only yesterday, Riis Park bustled
with laughter and WBLS blasted everywhere.
Beautiful bodies languished on the sand in
colorful swimwear. Volleyball players along with
joggers ran up and down. Lifeguards whistled
swimmers who strayed too far. Some vendors

hawked pepsi and ice-cream sandwiches. Others
hustled cheap cologne and fake gold braclets.
That day of wine and smiles, we were all walking
on sunshine.

Next to me on the 'I LOVE NEW YORK'
beach mat, dreads cascading down his head, Duke
eased through his one hundred daily push-ups.
Every inch of his six-foot taut body glistened
deliciously like honey. Many a passing glance
sized him up but the dude was all mine and had
been mine for ten years. He was so fine that I
paid no attention to a spot on his left foot, right
below his big toe; a spot, small, purple like the
stain of a crushed grape.

Soon after, it multiplied like stars in early
evening. Like buds on a tree in early spring, it
multiplied all over his feet, his legs, up his ass,
inside his intestines, all over his face, his neck,
down his throat, inside his brains. For nine
months of fever and wracking coughs, nine
months of sweat and shaking chills, nine months
of diarrhea and jerking spasms, they multiplied,
wrenched him skinny like a spider: a body of
pain.

'Sky, I don't understand this. I don't want to
understand this,' popped out of Duke as he came
out of the anesthesia. 'I'm sick of this hose in my
nose. I'm sick of this tube in my dick, all these
iv's in my arms. I'm sick of being strapped to this
bed.' He coughed out a scream.

'Easy, easy baby,' I whispered, smoothing my
gloved hand over his head, the side they hadn't
shaved for the biopsy, glad he was starting
trouble again. I bet he could see my smile behind
the mask they made me wear.

'I ain't joking. I am tired,' he said. 'I am
really tired and I'd rather be dead.'

'Sir Duke, don't you talk like that. You ain't

gonna die. You're only thirty-one, you're too young to die. We gonna beat this shit,' I kept repeating. 'That's why I want you to come home where you belong. One month is too freaking long to stay cooped up in this room. This hospital food ain't fit for a dog. I'm gonna make you strong. We gonna cheat death, you hear me. Sky and Duke hooked for life. Come on say it. Say it like we used to sing it all the time. Say it.'

'Sky,' he muttered, 'I'm gonna die.'

'No!' I kept yelling in the corridor, running to the nurses' station where three of them stood.

'Mr Carter, calm down. I told you so many times before that you should dispose of your gloves and your gown as soon as you leave the room,' the head nurse said as she rushed in Duke's room with another nurse.

'What's the number of the Administrator on Duty?' I asked this short Filipino nurse. 'I want to take my lover home.'

'Take him home, what do you mean?' she asked.

'I believe I'm speaking English. I said I want to take him home.'

'But your friend is dying. The biopsy showed Kaposi.'

'You are killing him. You and all this hospital ain't doing shit for him. Idiots! You should be ashamed of yourselves.'

'Mr Carter,' the head nurse said as she walked back, 'why don't you get some rest. You'll be doing your friend and yourself a disservice if you continue this vigil. Come on, sit down and drink some water.' She filled a paper cup and put it to my lips. 'It's alright,' she said. 'I understand,' and she held me.

From then on I wasted no time. Duke was too weak now but in a week he could be home.

He did consent after much convincing, insisting I take down all twelve mirrors hanging on every wall in the apartment. My indefinite leave of absence was approved quickly. Ever since I had told my co-workers about Duke's illness and why I had been so stressed, they've been wiping the unit's phone with alcohol. This year, they even asked me to bring liquor to the Christmas party instead of my tasty vegetable tempura.

I took a bank loan. Said it was for continuing education. I rented a wheelchair, a walker and a commode. I bought sheepskin pillows, a portable suction machine, a stand-up bed tray, hot water bottles, all kinds of medical supplies and bundles of paper towels. With coupons and Duke's foodstamps, I stacked up the refrigerator. I vacuumed, dusted and waxed the parquet floor. I called on friends to volunteer for chores. My sister Belzora, a retired Registered Nurse, said she'd come up from Georgia. Instead of a hard narrow bed in a sterile room, Duke would die in the dignity and beauty of his own home, on our big brass bed.

'Sir Duke, do you remember the first time we met at Peter Rabbit?' I asked him the night he came home as we sat on the living-room sofa, his head resting on my chest.

'How could I forget. You and your bunch of loud friends were bitching at the bar, singing all them old ballads so off-key. Sky you were stoned-drunk.'

'I was not. I was just enjoying a nice Sunday soiree and besides, you're the one who walked in them tight bell-bottom jeans and platform shoes, got everybody's heart pumping and jumping. Duke, you looked so good and when the d.j. played HOOKED FOR LIFE I had to ask you to dance.'

That night we sang, even danced a bit; two disco divas with ten years of memorabilia, the trips, the parties, the steps, the orgies...laughter.

'Sky,' he whispered as I tucked him in bed and kissed him goodnight, 'I'm glad I'm home. I love you. Thanks for the good times.'

Time was running out. Days went by. Duke made a will, named me executor of his estate. He couldn't get up or eat by himself. Belzora flew in like she had promised. She fixed all those deep-southern meals Duke used to like but could hardly eat. He'd stare at the wall with a glazed far-away look, eyes sunken way back.

Nights went by. He gagged, choked and vomited. I helped him sit up and cough, massaged his back, washed him up, changed his diapers, smoothed the bed sheets, caressed him until he fell asleep then woke up again from a nightmare, struggling for air. Every four hours, Belzora would give him shots of morphine to soothe the pain.

The doctor came in one day and said that he didn't expect Duke to live through the week. His mother Doris, his aunt Sylvia, his three brothers and their wives flew in from all over the country.

That Friday at 3.00 pm, while his aunt knelt at the foot of the bed, reading the twenty-third psalm, his mother seated on the bed held his left hand, and I, seated on the bed, held his right hand, trusting the instant, Duke yielded his soul.

There were no tears. There was no time for tears that year. Just a tight knot in the pit of my chest where it hurts more each day. Yet, it had all come to this: a two-pound plastic bag filled with a promise gone, scattered dreams, can't even pick up the pieces, all too quick.

## Epitaph


there's a grave in your heart
father holed
where over & over you lay
to bury yourself
through
thirty years of fits
furies & fangs
ground zero

*

here lives she
whose womb is a wound


## Triple Trouble


Last July 4th, like every July 4th for four years,
Nile ground ginger roots and lime rind, spooned
brown sugar in a cup of Cockspur rum he gulped.
Carrying on his head
all the front pages
           of New York Post for the past year
all the front pages
           with sorry stories
all the front pages
           with mad headlines
which had struck and hurt his eyes, he climbed
the stairs of his abandoned building on Eighth
Street between B & C. In the center of the cement
rooftop, he heaped the papers on which he
gracefully stripped. He rubbed greek-imported
olive oil over his body to catch more heat.

Staring straight at the sun
          Nile waited to hear the voice
staring straight at the sun
          Nile waited to feel the beat
staring straight at the sun
          Nile waited till his teeth clacked
with a shriek so hot it set the heap on fire. Round
and round the flames he ran, talking in tongues.
Then, on the roof's edge, he perched in arabesque
like an eagle ready for flight. High above his
head, he lifted his arms. In his fluttering fingers,
the sun shattered. The universe stood still while
Nile smiled. An empowering mystery, the past
passed on from generations, all the joy of life
reflected. So slowly his body bent far forward.
Long supple arms opened low
to pay homage
to surrender in prayer
to offer himself
          a black queen          dancing with shadows
                    at high noon
triple trouble that's brutal chasing America's evil
     spirits away.

*Gay Verse* from GMP, the Gay Men's Press

## SO LONG DESIRED
Poems by
James Kirkup & John McRae
ISBN 0-85449-038-8
64pp—UK £2.95/US $5.95

## DREAMS AND SPECULATIONS
Poems by
Paul Binding & John Horder
ISBN 0-85449-039-6
64pp—UK £2.95/US $5.95

## THREE NEW YORK POETS
Poems by
Mark Ameen, Carl Morse & Charles Ortleb
ISBN 0-85449-052-3
96pp—UK £3.95/US $7.95

## NOT LOVE ALONE
Martin Humphries (ed.)
Anthology of gay verse
by 30 modern gay poets
ISBN 0-85449-000-0
144pp—UK £3.50/US $6.50

## THE ANGEL OF DEATH
## IN THE ADONIS LOUNGE
Poems by
Marc Almond
ISBN 0-85449-079-5
64pp—UK£3.95/US $7.95